Cricket's Expeditions

Outdoor & Indoor Activities

by Kathleen Leverich

and the Editors of *Cricket Magazine*
Illustrated by Bob Totten

Random House New York

Library of Congress Cataloging in Publication Data

Leverich, Kathleen.   Cricket's expeditions.   Bibliography: p.   Summary:
Includes instructions for trailblazing, making secret codes and treasure maps, bird
watching, star gazing, and "grocery store" gardening.   1. Games—Juvenile literature.
2. Creative activities and seat work—Juvenile literature.   3. Recreation—Juvenile
literature.   [1. Recreation.   2. Games]   I. Totten, Bob.   II. Cricket.   III. Title.
GV1203.L469   790   77-3231   ISBN: 0-394-83543-3   ISBN: 0-394-93543-8 (lib. bdg.)

Manufactured in the United States of America   1 2 3 4 5 6 7 8 9 0

Contents

Cricket's Expeditions

Explorers search for buried treasure, ancient ruins, sunken ships, lost cities, uncharted rivers—and other things that are strange, exciting, and new to them. Their trips are called *expeditions*. That's what this book is filled with—directions for planning and taking strange, exciting expeditions. You are the explorer. You can begin anytime you like, and your expeditions won't take you farther away than your own home, your backyard, your neighborhood park or schoolyard.

But before you grab your knapsack and head for the door, you need to make some important preparations. The trip is only half an explorer's fun. The other half is reliving the expedition when it's over. Imagine sitting around a campfire or a blazing hearth and telling your friends and fellow explorers all about your daring deeds—while you toast marshmallows and drink hot chocolate. Now, that's the way to finish an expedition.

So, here's what you should do:

1. Keep notes, drawings, and photographs while you are on each expedition.

2. Organize an Explorer's Club. Any of your friends who go on expeditions may join. And you can have membership cards and a secret password. (Make it a Junior Explorer's Club. There's already one for adults from all over the world. Its headquarters in New York

City is full of maps, globes, leather armchairs, hunting trophies, and explorers who are between expeditions.)

    3. Have a meeting once a week. Take turns holding the meetings at each member's house. Serve hearty refreshments, relax in large squishy armchairs, and have one member give a report at each meeting. The report should be about that explorer's latest expedition. Other members can ask questions at the end. They might want advice or suggestions for going on similar expeditions of their own.

Trailblazing

Explorers have to think about many important things before they set out on expeditions. First they must decide what they are looking for—a fantastically frightful sea monster, an uncharted shortcut to the candy store, the lost continent of Atlantis, or the fabled Blue Rose of Bhutan that turns winter to summer and makes cold, gloomy people warm and friendly.

So when planning an expedition, first ask yourself: What am I looking for, and where shall I try to find it? Then, collect your supplies—maps, if you are going someplace that has already been explored; a compass, if you are venturing into uncharted regions; provisions, including plenty of fruit and cookies for quick energy; and—*extremely important*—something to mark your trail. That way, travelers who come after you will be able to follow your route. (That way, you will be able to find your way home!)

Here are some ways to mark your path:

1. Tie small pieces of string around branches, bushes, or rocks.

2. Dab small spots of yellow, orange, or red poster paint on rocks, leaves, or tree trunks. Use poster paint only; it comes off later.

3. Arrange twigs or rocks to point out your directions.

Do not use bread crumbs or any other kind of food to mark your trail. Remember what happened to Hansel and Gretel!

Now you are ready to set off on any expedition you choose. Just be sure to tell someone where you're going. Or, if you're not in the mood for a full-fledged expedition, what about trying this game?

The Fugitive and the Hunters

You can play this game with one or more friends or all by yourself. The idea is for one person, the fugitive, to run away and hide, leaving a trail behind. The other players, the hunters, give the fugitive a few minutes head start; then they pursue the runaway, trying to find and follow the trail.

The type of trail depends on where you play the game. In the dirt, the fugitive can erase his or her footprints by sweeping the path with a tree branch. In the snow, the fugitive can confuse the hunters by backtracking, stepping backward in footprints already made, and then—at a turnoff in the first path—heading in another direction. The hunters will find two trails and won't know which to follow. At the beach, the fugitive can make gaps in his or her footprints by occasionally walking through the water. At home, the fugitive can mark the trail with playing cards, paper clips, pieces of string, rubber bands, etc. And in the woods, the fugitive can leave a trail as suggested before.

Note: If you are playing by yourself, make the trail lead to a treasure!

Box lives

When we want to learn about people who lived three hundred or three thousand years ago, we look at the things they left behind. Sometimes we find paintings, palaces, ships, furniture, clothing, or—if we're especially lucky—a diary.

Diaries are better than royal proclamations or old newspapers for learning about the past. Can you guess why? Think about what you would write in a diary of your own. You'd tell what you're studying in school, who your friends are, and what games you play. You would probably write about what you like to eat and what you did on Halloween, your birthday, or New Year's Eve.

All those things might sound very ordinary to you, but how would they sound to people living three hundred years from now? They *could* sound very odd. "People were awfully silly in those days," your great-great-great-grandchild might say. "They stuck candles in everything from cakes to pumpkins, and they were always looking for an excuse to gobble up candies and cookies and ice cream."

Diaries tell about the little things we often don't even notice because we do them every day. But those are the things people from other times and places find the strangest. Diaries also tell about private feelings. And those don't change over the years. People long ago were frightened, happy, sad, brave, lonely, and loving—just as we are—and just as people in the future will be.

Unfortunately, there are not many old diaries to be found. Archaeologists, the scientists who study ancient people and cultures, usually find much simpler things —pottery bowls, weapons, the ruins of a temple, stone carvings. From these few objects they try to understand how the ancient people spent their days. (There is more about archaeology on page 39.)

One way to make things easier for the people who come after us is to keep a diary or journal. Another way is to make a *time capsule*. Time capsules are airtight containers that hold everything from photographs to eggbeaters to movies to toothpaste—all kinds of things we use every day. Current newspapers and books describing the latest fashions or the newest scientific discoveries are often put in. Then the time capsules are sealed and buried or cemented into the cornerstone of a building. When they are opened one hundred or one thousand years later, they tell what people of the past were like and how they lived.

You can make a time capsule of your own, called a Box Life. It will be about just you. Box Lives, like box lunches, can be made in any size or shape. You can use a shoe box, an old jewelry box, a cigar box, a heart-shaped candy box from last Valentine's Day, or a plastic storage box. Any box will do. Just be sure it is sturdy and not too big, or you will not be able to fill it up.

For your box, choose contents that tell something important about your life. Here are some suggestions:

1. Photographs or drawings of your family, house, town, and school.

This Box Life, Being the Souvenirs, Artifacts and observations of _____, was assembled and Sealed by me on _____ in the ___ year _____, of my life. Signed _____

2. An autobiography telling when and where you were born, what you have done since then, and what you want to do when you are older. Or a story about what you do on a typical day, from the time you get up in the morning until you go to bed at night.

3. A list of special places in your house—hiding places, secret compartments, the spot where the Christmas tree stands or where the dog sleeps.

4. A story about the most exciting moment in your life—or the scariest, the proudest, the most embarrassing, the happiest.

5. A recipe for your favorite dessert.

6. A list of your favorite things to do and friends to do them with.

7. Souvenirs—postcards, dolls, bottle cap collections, maps, theater programs, baseball trading cards.

8. An identification card. On a piece of heavy, official-looking paper, write:

This Box Life, being the souvenirs, artifacts, and observations of

_____, was assembled and sealed on _____ in the
(your name)   (date)

_____ year of my life. _____
(your age)   (your signature)

Place the identification card on top of everything else in the box. Put on the lid, and then seal the box with tape. If you want, you can wrap it up, too. In large numbers, print the year on the box top.

Now, put your Box Life away for posterity in the attic, the cellar, or the back of a dark closet. *Don't bury it;* the wet ground would probably ruin it.

In one year or five years or ten years you can take it out and peek inside. You may be surprised by what you find. You may even catch yourself saying, "What strange ideas and habits this long-ago person had!"

Bird detecting

Have you read any Sherlock Holmes mysteries, or have you seen the movie versions on television? If you have, you will remember that Holmes was able to solve the mysteries and become a master detective because he knew how and what to observe. He noticed and remembered all the small details that his friend Dr. Watson missed. When Holmes put all the little details together like the pieces of a jigsaw puzzle, he had a picture of the guilty character.

Detectives must always be good observers, but they don't always have to look for guilty characters. There are hundreds of other mysteries a good detective can solve.

John James Audubon was one kind of detective. He lived in the early 1800s and loved the outdoors. He went

on long hikes and camping trips by himself, and he always noticed the wildlife around him. Audubon was also a talented painter, and his favorite subjects were the birds he saw on his woodland trips. He learned to be quiet and still so he could note every detail of a bird's appearance before it flew away. He looked at its size, the color of its feathers, the shape of its head, tail, and wings. Then he was ready to paint.

But John James Audubon was more than a painter. He was a detective, too. He was curious about the birds he painted. Besides observing how they looked, he listened to their songs and made notes about where and when he saw each different bird. Then he spent long hours studying books about birds. He wrote to experts describing the birds he had seen and sending the paintings he had made of them.

Through his careful detective work, Audubon was able to find and count four hundred thirty-five different types of North American birds. Many were unknown anywhere else in the world, and Audubon discovered and named some himself.

You can be a bird detective, too. You can observe birds in a woods, in a park, or right in your own backyard. Here is the way to begin:

1. Choose a spot near your home. It can be a bird feeder in your yard, a patch of ground in a vacant lot, or a quiet spot in a park.

2. Visit that spot every day at the same time.

3. Leave birdseed, bread crumbs, or suet, and then sit down a little distance away where you can watch without disturbing your visitors.

4. Keep a pad or notebook handy so you can write short descriptions of the birds you see. Write down how

big they are—as big as your hand? Your foot? A squirrel? What colors are they? What shapes are their heads, tails, beaks, and wings? If it is easier, you can draw pictures as Audubon did.

5. Get a bird guidebook from your library and look through it until you find the birds that fit your descriptions. (Some good bird guides are listed at the end of this book.) Read about the birds to find out their mating and nesting habits, their migration patterns, and their diets.

6. After you identify all the birds, you might want to keep track of when you saw them. If you live in a cold climate, which birds stay around all year? Which birds are the first to return after the long winter? Write their names on a calendar.

Secret codes and private post offices

There are times when secrets are important, times when you must tell someone something without others understanding what you are saying. When you're planning a surprise party for your grandmother's birthday. Or when you're discussing what to get your brother for Christmas. Or when you and your brother are deciding how to replace the broken vase before your mother notices it. Or when you simply *must* talk to your best friend about private matters.

Soldiers, spies, and diplomats have had this problem for centuries. Especially in times of war, they need to tell their friends and allies secrets that their enemies must not hear. They have found a solution. They don't talk at all; they send messages written in code.

You can make up your own code for important private messages. Here are some suggestions for simple ways to begin:

1. Choose a color code. For example:

red = most important
yellow = good news
black = danger

You can write the whole message in the color that fits it.

Or you can just make a mark of that color on the message after you've folded it up. Now your friend will know what kind of news to expect just by looking at the note. If the mark is black, for example, he will know to hide before reading the message.

2. Choose key words and sentences. Then pick other words to replace them in your messages. For example:

For	Use
I must see you	giraffe
mother	rose
father	anchor
teacher	bell
call me on the phone	the sun is out
don't tell anyone	crocodiles like gumdrops
one or one o'clock	January
two or two o'clock	February
(and so on)	

Using this code, you could write: *Giraffe at May. The bell is talking to my rose today. The sun is out to say okay. Remember, crocodiles like gumdrops!* Your friend would

know you meant: *I must see you at five o'clock. The teacher is talking to my mother today. Call me on the phone to say okay. Remember, don't tell anyone.*

3. If you need to use words that are not part of your code, you can spell them backwards or scramble the letters. You should underline these words so that your friend will know to decode them.

4. Choose a place to use as a private post office. Then there will be less chance of your message falling into the wrong hands. Here are some possible private post offices: a tree hollow, a crack in a stone wall, a book that no one ever takes from its shelf, an envelope taped out of sight on the back wall of a closet.

5. As a final precaution, you can write in invisible ink! You will need:

a lemon or three tablespoons of ReaLemon Juice
a cup
a toothpick
a sheet of plain white paper

Squeeze all the lemon juice or pour the ReaLemon into a small cup. Using the toothpick as a pen, dip into the lemon juice and write your message on the paper. Be sure to keep the toothpick damp; dip it often into the lemon juice. When the juice dries, the writing disappears. To make the message visible, hold it close to something hot—a light bulb or a radiator or an iron. *Don't* use a match, a candle, or any other flame; your message may go up in smoke. As you slowly heat the paper, you will see brownish writing begin to appear.

Milk is also a good invisible ink. To make the writing visible again, rub it with graphite powder. (A pencil is made of graphite; scrape the lead part to get the powder.)

Mrs. Crabapple just told mom that I popped bubble gum during History class!

S.T.

Stained-glass windows

Stained-glass windows were among the most beautiful ornaments used to decorate churches in the Middle Ages. Constructing a window was a very long and difficult job because each step, even making the colored glass, had to be done by hand.

First a design for the window was prepared by an artist. Then the design was drawn again, as a pattern, exactly the same size as the finished window would be. The completed pattern was made up of sections that looked a little like the pieces of a jigsaw puzzle.

Each separate pattern section had to be carefully outlined and labeled with its proper color. Then glass of the matching color was laid over the pattern. The window makers could see the pattern lines through the glass, and they carefully cut the glass along the lines. Finally, the pattern was completely covered with small pieces of colored glass, each cut to the proper size and shape.

Now the picture was complete, but something was needed to hold all the pieces together. Lead was the best material to use. It would not weaken or decay, and it could be melted easily and poured between the glass sections. It bound them firmly when it cooled and hardened.

Last of all, an artist painted on any details that could not be shown simply with glass—such as the faces of saints and angels. Then the window was ready to be mounted in the church.

Stained-glass windows are still made today—but only a few. The craft is difficult, and the materials and labor are expensive; few people or organizations can afford them, and even fewer people can make a living producing them.

You can make your own version of a stained-glass window. It's not nearly as difficult and time-consuming as the real thing, but it will be just as beautiful.

You will need:

plain white paper	pencil
two sheets of black	scissors
construction paper	rubber cement
colored cellophane	paper clips

1. On the white paper, draw the outline of the picture you want in your window. It should be very simple. Then draw heavy lines to divide the picture into sections. As you work, remember that every line is a strip of lead, and every section is a separate piece of glass. This is a difficult project, so you may want to use the pattern on pages 24-25 for your first picture. Trace this pattern onto the white paper; then follow the rest of the directions. When you have finished, you will have a good idea of just how all the materials fit together. Then you can design your own window.

2. Look carefully at the pattern. You will see that each pattern section is outlined in black, and the black lines are all connected. They are not broken anywhere.

3. Decide what colors you want the sections to be and label each one with the name of the color you've chosen.

4. Using a pair of small, sharp, pointed scissors, carefully cut out all the sections that should be colored. Everything will be cut away except the connecting lines of "lead." *Important*: Do *not* cut across any of the black "lead" lines, and do *not* damage the colored sections as you cut them out. You will need them later.

5. When you have cut out all the sections, you will have a pattern of the outlines of your picture.

6. Place the pattern on top of one of the sheets of black paper. (The black paper is going to be your win-

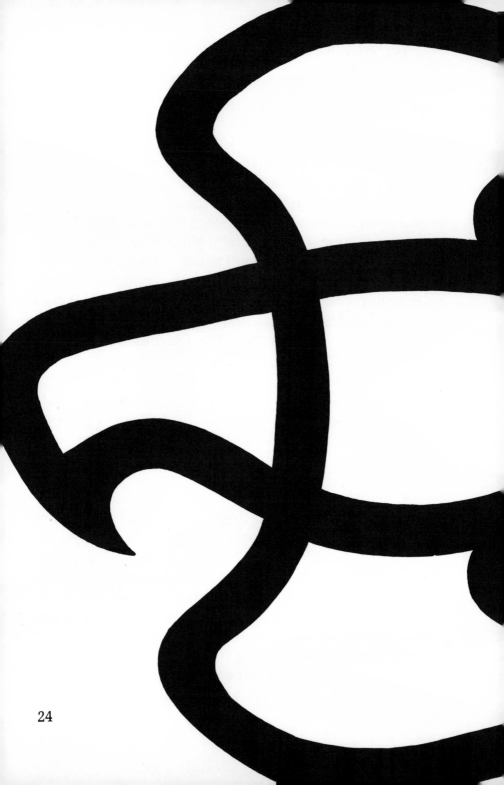

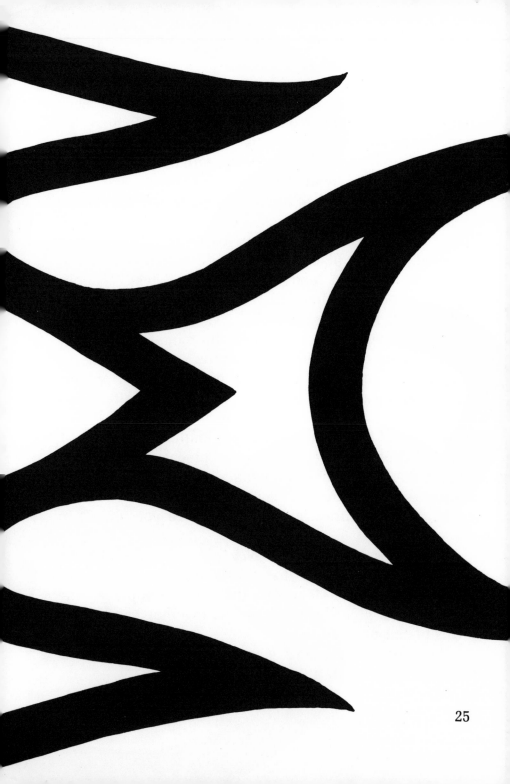

dow's lead.) Paper clip the two sheets of paper firmly together at each corner.

7. Using the top white sheet as a stencil, trace around the "lead" lines so that the outlines of each pattern section appear on the black sheet. Remove the paper clips and separate the two sheets of paper. Cut out the pattern sections you just drew, again being careful not to cut across the "lead" lines.

8. Paper clip the white outline pattern to the second sheet of black paper. Trace the design onto the black paper and cut out the pattern sections. When you're finished, the two black sheets should match exactly.

9. Now you're ready to cut out the "glass" sections of your window. Collect all the pattern sections you cut from the original window design. (They're the ones made of white paper and labeled with the names of colors.)

10. Place each pattern section on cellophane of the proper color and carefully cut around it. *Important*: As you cut, allow a half-inch border around each pattern section. In other words, the cellophane must be one-half inch larger, *on all sides*, than the paper pattern.

11. When all the cellophane pieces are cut out, choose one black sheet and place each piece over the pattern section it should fill. The cellophane will overlap onto the "lead" lines, and that is where you glue it in place.

12. Allow the glue to dry. Now place the second black sheet over the first so that the cellophane pieces are sandwiched inside. Make sure that the cutout places line up, and then glue the black sheets together around the edges of the paper.

13. When the glue is dry, your stained-glass picture is ready to hang up in a window.

26

Ecologist's notebook

Millions of kinds of plants, animals, fish, insects, birds, and reptiles live on this earth. Each kind is different from the others, but in many ways they are all the same. They are all living things, and they all depend on each other to continue living. This balance, or relationship, between living things is what ecologists study. The word *ecology* comes from the Greek language and means "knowledge of the household." The household is the earth, shared by all forms of life.

You can be an ecologist, too, by studying the relationships of the plants and animals in your own backyard

or in a nearby park or vacant lot. This is what you do to make an Ecologist's Notebook:

1. Take a large sheet of construction paper or poster board. Using a ruler, divide the sheet into nine vertical and eight horizontal sections. You should end up with seventy-two blocks.

2. Beginning with the second block from the top,

	Trees	Plants	Animals	Birds	Insects	Weather	Misc.	Chains
Mon.								
Tues.								
Wed.								
Thurs.								
Fri.								
Sat.								
Sun.								

label the blocks in the far left vertical column: Monday, Tuesday, Wednesday, Thursday, Friday, Saturday, and Sunday.

3. Beginning with the second block from the left, label the blocks in the top horizontal column: Trees, Plants, Animals, Birds, Insects, Weather Conditions, Miscellaneous, and Chains. Your chart should look something like the one on page 28.

4. Go on a nature hike. Bring a pad of paper, a pencil, and a pocket guidebook about trees and plants. (Some good ones are listed in the back of this book; you can get them at the library.) Go around the block, into the park, up and down your street, backyard, or neighborhood. Spend at least fifteen minutes looking around.

5. Keep notes on the kinds of trees, plants, birds, animals, insects, etc., that you see. Also note the weather conditions and the time of day.

6. When you get home, transfer your observations to the proper blocks on your chart.

7. Most important, try to connect the things you see. For example, if you see a rosebush blooming in a flower bed and then see a worm in the same soil, think: How does the worm affect the rose? Well, as the worm crawls through the soil, it loosens and breaks up the dirt so it will absorb more water and the rose can push its roots through more easily. The worm also fertilizes the soil so the rose has food to grow. This relationship should be listed in the "Chains" column.

The worm and the rose make one link in a growing life chain. The next link may be a bee that gathers nectar from the rose and takes it back to the hive to make into honey. Or it may be an aphid that eats the rosebush and, in turn, becomes food for a hungry bird. Sometimes you won't see the relationships until you have gone home and studied your notes.

8. Every week, begin a new chart.

9. You can carry a magnifying glass on your walks. Look at wild flowers, plant leaves, and insects through the glass. Sketch them on your pad.

10. When you get home, paste your sketches on a piece of colored construction paper. Label them with their names. Keep the sketches together in a folder or loose-leaf notebook.

11. Collect interesting or pretty things you find on your walks—brightly colored autumn leaves, bird feathers, eggshells, and seashells. Add them to your notebook or to a nature shelf. Here is a way to mount the leaves:

Put a leaf on a piece of colored paper and cover it with waxed paper. Put a dishtowel on the ironing board. Holding the colored and waxed papers tightly together, turn them over and lay them on the dishtowel. Turn on the iron at its lowest setting and press the entire piece of paper several times. Turn the paper over. The heat from the iron will have melted the wax, and the waxed paper and colored paper will be firmly stuck together with the leaf handsomely mounted in between.

12. Make bark rubbings. You'll need:

a soft pencil, a stick of charcoal, or a piece of colored chalk
a piece of white paper (not too thick)
four thumbtacks

Choose a tree with smooth bark to begin. You can try rougher barks like oak and elm when you are more experienced. Attach each corner of your paper to the tree with a thumbtack. Turn your pencil sideways and rub the lead across the paper with even, gentle strokes. Take the paper off the tree. Label it and put it in your Ecologist's Notebook next to the leaves you have sketched and collected and waxed from that tree.

Favorite files

Have you ever thought about what you would wish for if a mysterious genie granted you one wish? Sometimes you don't even have to think. You know right away just exactly what will make you happiest. But other times you might not be so sure. There are so many things to choose from —a ten-speed bike, a puppy, a birthday every week, a trip around the world on an elephant. Choosing can be hard, but there is something much worse. Not being able to think of anything to wish for at all!

You probably won't have a chance to tell a genie your wish, so don't worry about that. But there are other times when you *do* have a chance to choose. And times when you can't remember what you want. For example, your father says, "I'm going to stop for ice-cream cones. What flavor do you want?" And you can't remember that flavor you liked so much last time. (Mango-banana-crunchy-chip-ripple?)

Or what about evenings in the shower or the bathtub? You open your mouth wide to belt out a hearty tune, and you can't remember even *one* good bathtub song.

Or in the library? It's going to be a cold rainy night; you and your parents are going to build a fire in the fireplace and pop some corn. The only thing missing is an exciting book, and you can't remember the names of any of the mysteries your friends told you were terrific.

To avoid these problems, this is what you can do:

Keep lists of good or favorite things. Then you will be prepared in case of emergencies in the ice-cream parlor, the shower, the library, or anywhere else. Here are some suggestions for lists you might want to keep:

   songs
   books
   games
   happy thoughts
   movies
   places to visit within walking distance
   places to visit farther away
   snacks
   things to do on rainy days
   jokes and riddles
   what you're going to be when you grow up (adults are always asking about this, so you might as well have an answer)

It's fun to see how your favorites change and to compare your lists with your friends' lists. You can make a notebook and set aside one page for each list. Or you can list your favorites on file cards and collect them in a box that you have decorated. Or you can write each list on a small pad that you carry with you—the book list to the library, the song list to the tub.

And, you might want to keep a list of good things to wish for . . . just in case.

Treasure maps

Treasure maps have been famous throughout history for causing greed, suspicion, and murder. Remember the Captain's map in *Treasure Island*, the maps grave robbers used when they broke into Egyptian pyramids, and the maps of sunken treasure ships in the Caribbean.

You can make a treasure map, too. It will be secret and exciting and show treasures as important to you as the treasures that cutthroats have murdered for—but no

one will murder for your map, because your treasures will be the sort that are best when they're shared.

Here is what you do:

1. Choose a large sheet of paper, oak tag, poster board, or cloth for your map. (Cloth will look more genuinely old and mysterious.)

2. Begin by drawing a square in the middle of the map to show where your house is. Label it *home.*

3. In one corner of the map, make a circle with four compass points. Mark them *north* on top, *south* on the bottom, *east* on the right, *west* on the left.

4. Now, on a separate piece of paper, make two lists. One should include all your favorite places in your town or neighborhood: hiding places, the bakery, the baseball diamond, the ice skating pond, the movie theater, the field where you won a race, the park where you have picnics. The other list should include danger spots: the house of a ferocious dog, a swamp or a ditch, a poison ivy patch. It may take a few days to think of all the things that should go on the lists.

5. When your lists are complete, get your map and mark each treasure or danger spot where it belongs in the town. Use stars, circles, or hearts for the treasure spots. Use x's or skulls and crossbones for the danger spots.

6. Now choose one or two landmarks near each treasure and danger spot: a lake, a church, a school, a graveyard, a hill, a library, a large tree. Mark the landmarks by drawing small simple pictures of them on the map.

7. Now you must visit each landmark and find the distance between it and the treasure spot. For example, 10 paces north and 26 paces west. Keep notes as you go.

8. Go home and write the notes on the map next to each landmark.

9. Fold or roll up the map and hide it in your room. Use it as a guide when you want to hide something from your younger brother, when you play pirates with your friends, or when you have a scavenger hunt.

Do-it-yourself digs

Archaeologists, like most scientists, are detectives. They find, preserve, and study small clues, trying to solve ancient mysteries about how people lived long ago.

To investigate their mysteries, archaeologists often go to the faraway places where ancient people first lived and built homes and cities—Egypt, Kenya, China, Peru, Greece, and Mexico. Often they have no more than a battered hammer head or a broken pottery bowl for a clue. But the discoveries they make are sometimes fabulous—palaces, treasure-filled tombs, or whole cities, preserved just as they were thousands of years ago. Those were the discoveries that awaited Arthur Evans, Howard Carter, and Henry Layard, the men who found the lost kingdom of Knossos, the tomb of King Tut, and the ancient city of Nineveh.

Archaeologists usually have to dig for their discoveries. When a building is abandoned or a city deserted, it falls into ruins and is buried under shifting sands, flooded by rivers, or overgrown with forests or jungles. Often other people will return, decades or even hundreds of years later, to build a new city on top of an old one. For example, when workers in London were tearing up streets in 1954, they came upon a building buried deep below the city. It was a temple built by the Romans, who had ruled Britain two thousand years earlier.

Many things did not last the centuries between ancient times and the present. If exposed to the weather, food, wood, paper, leather, and wool turn to dust and vanish. But some things remain—pottery, stone or metal tools, ornaments of gold and silver, bones, and buildings. From these, archaeologists try to guess how ancient people looked and lived.

You can be a backyard archaeologist and discover extraordinary ruins from the past. But you must make some ruins and clues to discover, first.

1. Choose the type of civilization you want to discover: an ancient Mayan or Aztec city in the jungles of Central America or Mexico, an Egyptian pyramid, a Greek or Roman imperial city, the cave of prehistoric people who hunted mammoth and wild boar and painted pictures on their cave walls.

2. Visit the library and read about the civilization you have chosen. What kind of houses did they live in? How did they dress, and what tools did they use? Did they leave behind a written language, precious jewelry, or art objects?

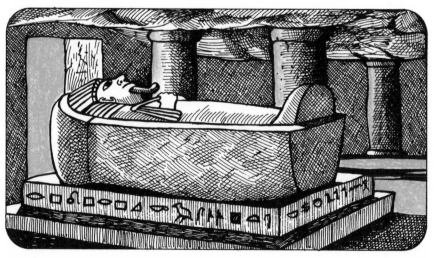

3. Now make or find the clues: broken pots, old shoes or sandals, stones that might be weapons or tools. You can even use bones from dinner, after they have been cleaned and dried. You might want to make up your own ancient language, write a message, and wrap it up or hide it so that it could have been preserved through the centuries. (The ancient Egyptians, for example, used hieroglyphics—a kind of picture writing—and wrote on parchment, sheepskin cured and used as paper.)

4. Stones piled in interesting arrangements could be the remains of temple pillars or palace steps or the foundation of a fortress wall. Trees can be historic sacred shrines. Coins collected from other countries can be ancient money.

5. If you want, you can even search for an imaginary civilization. After all, one of the most famous archaeologists, Heinrich Schliemann, discovered a city everyone thought was a myth and a dream. He discovered Troy.

Large-as-life likenesses

How many times a day do you look in a mirror? When you walk by a big store window, do you sneak a look at your reflection going by? And how about photographs? Lots of people complain that they just *hate* to have their picture taken. But do they really mean it? Probably not. Most people like to see images or pictures of themselves. Think of all the portraits, photographs, home movies, or mirrors you see in just one day.

Sometimes it's surprising to see a picture of yourself. You don't look at all the way you expected. You are blinking and wearing a silly grin. Or your eyes are turned up to heaven, your mouth is open, and you look like a surprised fish. Have you ever seen a stranger walking toward you and then realized it was really you—your image in a mirror?

You can make a likeness of yourself that shows you just as you want to be seen—at your very best. Here is what you'll need:

> heavy brown wrapping paper
> (the kind that comes in long rolls)
> scissors
> poster paints, crayons, or felt-tip pens

1. Cut a length of wrapping paper about one foot longer than your height.

2. Spread the paper flat on the floor and lie on it, face up. Ask your mother, father, or friend to draw around you, carefully and accurately.

3. Using the paints, crayons, or pens, fill in the outline by coloring your face, hair, and clothes.

4. When the paint or ink has dried, cut out the finished likeness and hang it on your closet door, bedroom wall, or anyplace else you like. You can make other outlines of yourself and use them to create imaginary friends from other times and places. Or make outlines of your real friends. Next year, and the year after, you can make a new life-sized likeness of yourself. That way you can see how you grow and change.

Grocery store gardening

Did you ever think as you spit out orange, cherry, or peach pits that you were throwing away the makings for a big, beautiful indoor garden? You can't grow fruit-bearing trees in your house, but you can raise miniature trees if you save the seeds and plant them and care for them properly. Here are some plants that grow easily indoors:

lemon
orange
pumpkin
squash
avocado
pea
watermelon
peach
bean

There are many ways to start your plant. The easiest works well for pumpkins, squash, fresh peas, lemons, oranges, and melons.

1. Find a flowerpot, a can, or a milk carton with the top cut off. Punch a few tiny holes in the bottom. Fill your container two-thirds full of potting soil (from the dime store) or dirt from your yard.

2. Sprinkle several of the seeds or peas on the soil.

3. Cover with more soil—about two inches or enough to fill the container. Press down the dirt, but don't pack it too hard or the plants won't be able to break through it when they start growing.

4. Water until a few drops seep out of the holes in the bottom of the container.

5. Place on a windowsill or any other sunny spot and check every day to make sure the soil is moist. Water lightly if it's not. Your plants should begin to sprout in five to ten days.

To start larger seeds such as avocados and peaches, try to find a pit that has already begun to split. This means that the plant roots and stem are beginning to push their

way out. Split seeds may be planted right away. Cover
them with a thin layer of soil; then water and place in the
sun. If you can't find a seed that has split, try to use one
from a fruit that hasn't been refrigerated. Then follow
these directions:

1. Set the seed in a cup or shallow bowl. Fill the cup
with enough water to cover the bottom, or rounded part,
of the seed.

2. Place in the sun and wait for roots to sprout.

3. When roots begin to grow, plant the seed in a pot,
as described earlier.

Sweet potatoes are fun to grow, too. The plants last
only a few weeks, but they grow quickly and have pretty
trailing vines.

1. Slice a raw sweet potato in half and place it, cut
side down, in a shallow dish of water. Do not cover the
whole potato with water.

2. Place the dish in a warm spot out of direct sunlight.

3. Your plant will begin to sprout tiny green leaves in
seven to ten days. Check the plant regularly and add
water to keep the water level the same.

Laundry bag lady

Where do you usually put your dirty clothes? In a hamper? At the back of your closet? In a heap on the floor? How would you like to give them to your own personal Laundry Bag Lady? Here's how to make her:

1. Ask your mother to save the next dress you wear out or outgrow or to give you an old dress of hers, your sister's, or your cousin's.

2. Turn the dress inside out and lay it flat on the floor or a table. Pin the front and back together along the skirt hem.

3. Now, using the tiniest stitches you can make, sew the front and back together where you pinned them. Remove the pins.

4. Sew across the hem two more times to make sure the stitching will hold. Turn the dress right side out.

5. Ask your mother for an old stocking and stuff the foot with foam rubber, paper, or scraps of material until it is round like a head.

6. Tie the stocking tightly, just above the foot, with string or ribbon. Then cut off the leg of the stocking about two inches above the string.

7. Using buttons, felt, yarn, and string, sew a face and hair on the stocking head. If hair is too difficult to make, you can put an old hat on the head instead.

8. Now get a spare clothes hanger. Bind the tied part of the stocking head to the hanger, at the base of the hook. Put the dress on the hanger, and you have made yourself a Laundry Bag Lady.

9. Hang the Laundry Bag Lady in your closet and unbutton or unzip her dress to put your dirty clothes inside. When she gets fat, it's time to do the wash!

Book jackets

When you are choosing a book at the library or in a bookstore, what do you look at first? Probably the jacket. The picture and colors on a book jacket can tell you a lot about what you will find inside. And, if you open the book, you will see that the inside flaps of the jacket tell you even more about the book. There are a few short paragraphs describing the story, the characters, the setting, or the subject. Very often the back flap has a picture and a brief history, or biography, of the author.

You may own some books that have lost their jackets. You can make new ones so that the books will be more exciting to look at. Book jackets also protect books from dirt and damage.

Here is what you do:

1. Choose the book you want to cover and find a piece of paper for the jacket. You may use any kind of paper that will fold easily—brown wrapping paper, shelf paper, tissue paper, or construction paper.

2. Open the book and lay it flat on the paper. The paper should be several inches larger than the book on all four sides.

3. Fold the top of the paper along the top edge of the book. Fold the bottom of the paper along the bottom edge of the book. Remove the book and fold the top and bottom

flaps flat to the inside. Your paper should now be the same height as the book.

4. Wrap the paper around the closed book so that the edges that overlap at the front and back of the book are even. Then fold the overlapping edges of paper inside the front and back covers. These will be the jacket flaps.

Now you are ready for the best part—designing the cover. Here are some possibilities:

1. Decide where on the jacket front you want the title of the book, the name of the author, and the cover picture to go.

2. Look through old holiday greeting cards and old magazines for a picture that fits the subject of your book. Cut out the picture and glue it to the front of your book jacket. As you sort through the cards and magazines, you might want to cut out other pictures that look interesting. Save them in a box or envelope so you will have them whenever you design a new book jacket.

3. You can use a family photograph as a cover picture. Sometimes they can be funny. For example, if you

were making a jacket for Laura Ingalls Wilder's book *The Long Winter*, you might choose a photograph of your family making a snowman.

Important: Before you use any cards, magazines, or photographs, check with your parents to make sure it's all right.

4. You can draw your own jacket picture, using crayons, felt-tip pens, paints, or colored pencils.

5. You can make interesting and unusual covers by using a combination of cards, magazine pictures, photographs, and drawings.

6. On the front and the spine, or side, of the jacket, print the title and author's name in large letters. If you like, you can write a bit about the book on the front jacket flap. And, in small letters at the bottom of the flap, you can write: Jacket designed by _____
(your name)

Star gazing

Long ago, people knew very little about the sky. The ancient Greeks and Romans, for example, believed the sky was a clear dome that rested on earth's flat horizon, that the stars were somehow attached to the dome, and that Diana—goddess of the moon—and Apollo—god of the sun—rode across it each night and day. They also thought that there were places, at the ends of the earth, where the dome touched the ground. If a person could journey to those places, they reasoned, he or she could touch the dome or perhaps even make a hole in it and look out at what lay beyond the sky.

Other ancient people had different ideas about what the stars and heavens were made of, but they all noticed and agreed on one thing. The stars were dependable; they appeared in the same groups each night.

Sailors, traders, and other travelers learned to navigate by the stars. They knew which groups of stars shone in the northern sky, which in the southern, eastern, and western skies.

To make the star groups easier to find, and perhaps to amuse themselves, travelers gave names to the groups, or *constellations* (*con* meaning "together," and *stella* meaning "stars"). There were: Pegasus the Winged Horse, Orion the Hunter, Draco the Dragon, Cancer the Crab,

Leo the Lion, Taurus the Bull, Bootes the Herdsman, Virgo the Virgin, Sagittarius the Archer, Cygnus the Swan, and many others.

The pictures on pages 55-57 show how some of the constellations appear in the night sky. The connecting lines show how the ancient Greeks and Romans pictured them.

With so many thousands of stars visible in the sky, it is a bit difficult to find constellations the first few times you try. But you will get better as you star gaze. In time you may see planets, shooting stars (these are actually meteors), comets, lunar halos, and eclipses, as well as the constellations. Who can tell? You might even sight a U.F.O.*

Here is how to begin star gazing:

1. Find out from your parents or from a compass which direction is north. On the next clear moonless night, go outdoors, face north, and look for the Big Dipper. It will look like this:

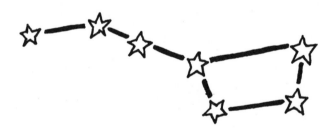

2. Now look at the two stars that make the outer side of the dipper's cup. In your mind, join them with a line. Follow that line up to the next bright star, and you have found the North Star. It always appears in the north, so it is very useful for navigation.

*Unidentified flying object

3. Now look for the Little Dipper. The end of the handle is the North Star, and the handle bends back toward the Big Dipper.

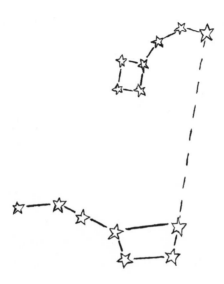

4. Another easy constellation to locate is Orion. In the winter, it is in the southern sky and looks like this:

5. Visit the library and find a guidebook to help you recognize more constellations. The guide will tell you what to look for and where to look at different times of the year. Some helpful star guides are listed at the end of this book.

6. Keep a chart, calendar, or notebook, and list: what you see in the sky each night, how long you star gaze, and what the weather is like. You will be surprised at how quickly the list of constellations you can find will grow.

Library scavenger hunt

Libraries are filled with all the stories, facts, figures, and dreams that people have wanted to share over the centuries. The first library was built over 2,500 years ago in the ancient kingdom of Assyria. There were no books in those days; there wasn't even any paper. Laws and great events were recorded by marking moist clay tablets. Then the tablets were dried and stored in the library. Carrying more than one page at a time was hard work!

Now libraries are filled with books, magazines, newspapers, records, films, and even microfilms, so that more and more information can be stored. You can go to the library and find a science-fiction story about life on Mars, a ten-year-old newspaper weather forecast, an arti-

cle about snakes in the Amazon jungle, or a recipe for peach ice cream.

To take library materials home, you need a library card. If you don't have one, ask your school or public librarian how to get one. Usually, it's as easy as signing your name.

Once you have a library card, you are ready to start choosing books. You can look for your favorite author or find books your friends have enjoyed, or you can ask the librarian for the names of good books on a subject that interests you. All the books are kept in a special order so people can find them easily. Picture books are in one section, fairy tales in another; baseball books, animal stories, and history books all have their own special places.

The key to finding these places is the *card catalog*. It is a kind of file cabinet, full of cards. In fact, there is at least one card in the catalog for every book in the library! The librarian can show you how the catalog works. After you have explored the library a few times and have looked through the catalog, you will make more and more exciting discoveries of treasures hiding on the library shelves.

To help you explore the library's treasures, try this Library Scavenger Hunt.

1. Look at the list of *Books for Planning Further Expeditions* on page 62.

2. Decide which expeditions you liked best—*Box Lives, Star Gazing, Do-It-Yourself Digs?*

3. Check the books listed under those expeditions and try to find them in the library. Use the card catalog or ask the librarian for help if you need to. Your library may not have all the books listed, but it should have others on the same subjects.

4. How many were you able to find? Did you discover any interesting books you weren't looking for? Did you learn where to find other books on the same subject?

5. From now on, before you go to the library, make a list of things to look for—last year's October issue of *Cricket*, a record album of Christmas carols, a storybook about horses or football or the American Revolution, a how-to book about mountain climbing or ice fishing or building a dugout canoe. Even if you decide not to take out the book, you will have learned more about libraries and books during your scavenger hunt.

If you become a real bibliophile, or book lover, and a confirmed library scavenger, you may want to set up your own library at home. Decide how to organize the books. You can arrange them in alphabetical order by author's name or by title, or you can group them according to subject—fairy tales, science, sports, natural history, true adventure, for example. For each book, write the title of the book, the name of the author, and the group on an index card. You can even add a few sentences describing what the book is about. Then put your books on the shelves in order. The cards can be kept in alphabetical order in a file box. Whenever you get a new book, you can add a card and place the book in its proper place on your shelves.

Books for planning further expeditions

Trailblazing
The Authorized Autumn Charts of the Upper Red Canoe River Country: Peter Z. Cohen
A Field Guide to Animal Tracks: Olaus Murie
The First Book of Animal Signs: C. B. Colby
How to Be a Nature Detective: Millicent Selsam

Box lives
The Diary of an Early American Boy: Noah Blake 1805: Eric Sloan
People and Places: Margaret Mead

Bird detecting
Bird Watchers and Bird Feeders: Glenn O. Blough
Birds and Their Nests: Olive L. Earle
The Birds of America: John James Audubon
A Field Guide to Western Birds: Rodger Tory Peterson
John James Audubon: Margaret Kieran

The National Audubon Society has many books and programs for people interested in birds. It also sponsors a Junior Audubon Society that you may want to join. Write to the society at: 950 Third Avenue, New York, New York 10022.

Secret codes and private post offices
"The Adventure of the Dancing Men" from *The Complete Sherlock Holmes*: Arthur Conan Doyle
Codes, Ciphers, and Secret Writing: Martin Gardner
The First Book of Codes and Ciphers: Sam and Beryl Epstein
"The Goldbug" from *Stories and Poems*: Edgar Allen Poe

Stained-glass windows
The First Book of Glass: Sam and Beryl Epstein
Jewels for a Crown: Miriam Freund
Made in the Middle Ages: Christine Price
Stained Glass Crafting: Paul W. Wood

Ecologist's notebook
Flowers: Herbert S. Zim and Alexander C. Martin
Path of Hunters: Robert Newton Peck
Sea and Earth: The Life of Rachel Carson: Phillip Sterling
Secret Neighbors: Mary Adrian
The Secret World: Mary DeBall Kwitz
Trees: Herbert S. Zim and Alexander C. Martin

Favorite files
Favorite Tales of Long Ago: James Baldwin
The Fireside Book of Folk Songs: Margaret Boni and Norman Lloyd
Half Magic: Edward Eager
A Book of Sorcerers and Spells: Ruth Manning-Sanders

Treasure maps
The First Book of Maps: Sam Epstein
Treasure Island: Robert Louis Stevenson

Do-it-yourself digs
The First Book of Archaeology: Nora B. Kubie
In the Land of Ur: Hans Baumann
Kon Tiki: Thor Heyerdahl
The Living Sea: Jacques-Yves Cousteau
Lost Worlds: Anne Terry White

Large-as-life likenesses
Famous Paintings: Alice Elizabeth Chase
The First Book of Mirrors: Sam and Beryl Epstein
Mirror on the Wall: Phillip B. Carona

Grocery store gardening
The Carrot Seed: Ruth Krauss
The First Book of Gardening: Helene Carter
Indoor Gardening Fun: R. Milton Carlton

Laundry bag lady
Clothes Tell a Story: Cecil and Winifred Lubell

Book jackets
Collage: Mickey K. Marks
Printmaking: Harlow Rockwell

Star gazing
A Field Guide to the Stars and Planets: Donald Mendel
Stars: Herbert S. Zim and Robert H. Baker
The Stars: A New Way to See Them: H. A. Rey

Library scavenger hunt
Books: A Book to Begin On: Susan Bartlett
Libraries: A Book to Begin On: Susan Bartlett